THE GIANT'S BREAKFAST

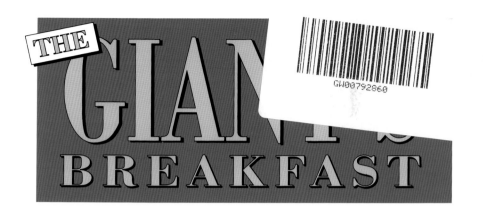

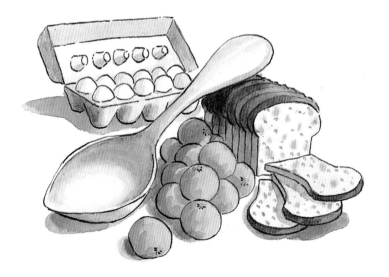

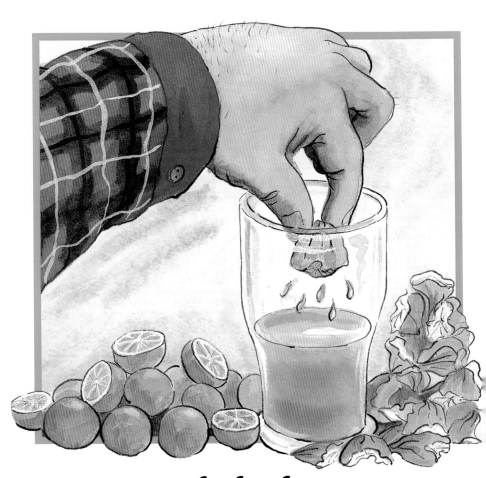

Fe-fi-fo-fum!
I smell oranges.

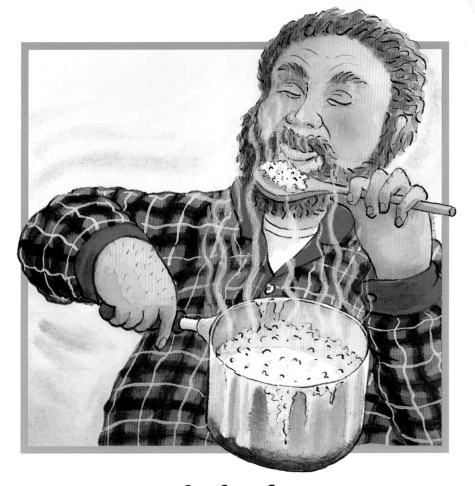

Fe-fi-fo-fum!
I smell oatmeal.

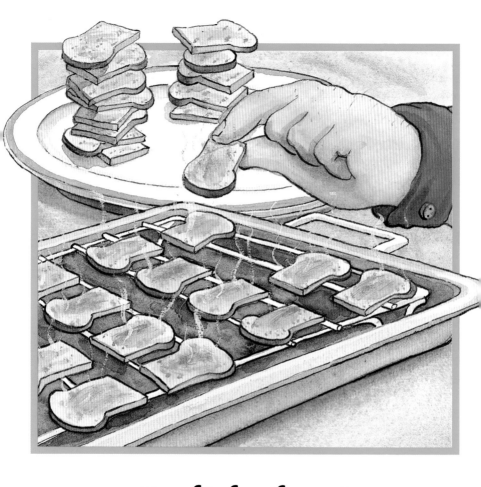

Fe-fi-fo-fum!
I smell toast.

4

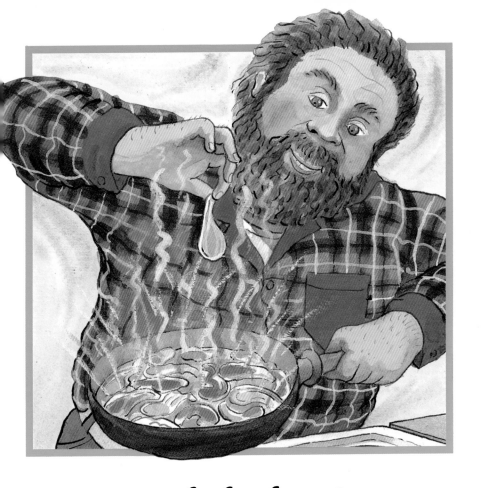

Fe-fi-fo-fum!
I smell ham.

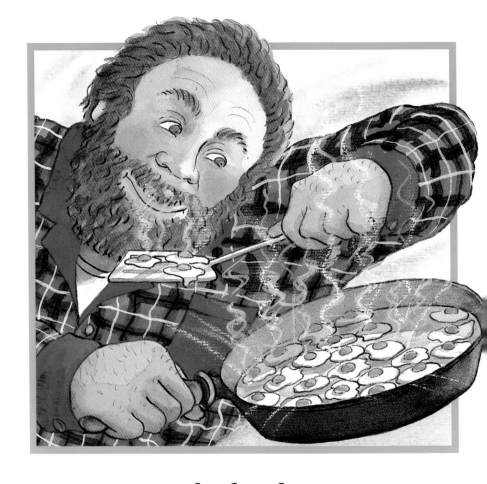

Fe-fi-fo-fum!
I smell eggs.

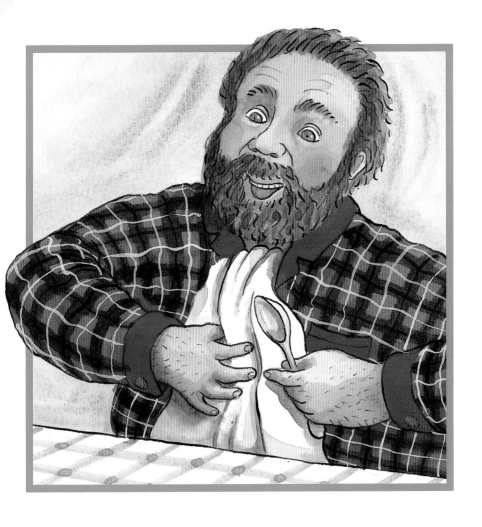

Fe-fi-fo-fum!

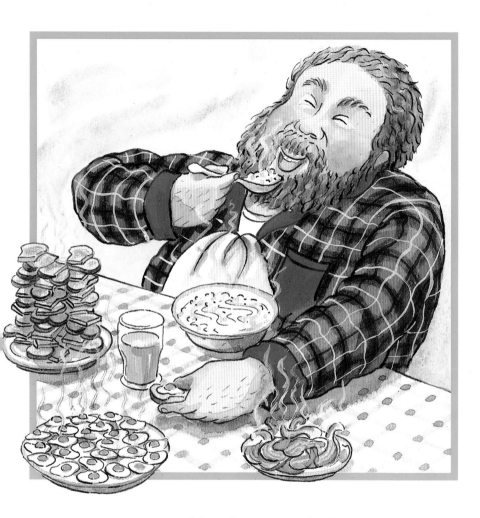

I smell breakfast!